Passed to Kelly's mother
from Meagan's mother
(Meagan married 6/20/15)

Mother of the Bride

also by Ilene Beckerman

Love, Loss, and What I Wore
What We Do for Love
Makeovers at the Beauty Counter of Happiness

Mother of the Bride

written and illustrated by
Ilene Beckerman

Algonquin Books of Chapel Hill
2005

Published by
Algonquin Books of Chapel Hill
Post Office Box 2225
Chapel Hill, North Carolina 27515-2225

a division of Workman Publishing
708 Broadway
New York, NY 10003

First paperback edition, Algonquin Books of Chapel Hill, April 2005.
Originally published by Algonquin Books of Chapel Hill in 2000.
Printed in Mexico.
Published simultaneously in Canada by Thomas Allen & Son Limited.

Library of Congress Cataloging-in-Publication Data

Beckerman, Ilene, 1935–
    Mother of the bride: the dream, the reality, the search for a perfect dress/
    written and illustrated by Ilene Beckerman.
        p. cm.
    ISBN 1-56512-259-3
    1. Weddings—Planning—Case studies. 2. Weddings—Planning—Humor.
    3. Mothers and daughters—Case studies. 4. Mothers and daughters
    —Humor. I. Title.

HQ745 .B43 2000
395.2'2—dc21   99-088845

ISBN 1-56512-476-6 (paper)

10 9 8 7 6 5 4 3 2 1
First Paperback Edition

"The daughter is for the mother at once her double and another person. . . ." Simone de Beauvoir, *The Second Sex*

DEDICATED TO MY DAUGHTERS

Mother of the Bride

All mothers want their daughters to get married.

To most mothers, a daughter in a marriage that's just okay is better than a daughter who's single and happy.

Still, as much as we want our daughters to be married, no woman is prepared for being the mother of the bride. I should know. I've married off three daughters.

To tell you the truth, childbirth was easier than being the mother of the bride.

The first wedding I ever went to was my cousin Sally's. I was ten. I'd only seen Sally twice. She came from the wrong side of the family. I didn't know why we were invited, but I did hear someone say, "If you invite one second cousin, you have to invite all the second cousins."

The next wedding I remember was at the Loew's movie theater on East 72nd Street in Manhattan. It was 1947 and there was a film clip of Elizabeth II marrying Lieutenant Philip Mountbatten on the Pathé News Reel.

My mother-of-the-bride story begins with the conception of my daughter, which took about five seconds; briefly covers my pregnancy, which took the usual nine months; and ends with the planning of my daughter's wedding, which took a year.

Forty years later, planning my daughter's wedding, I
remembered that film clip and wondered if the Queen
Mother had as many headaches when her first daughter
Elizabeth married Philip of Greece as I had when my first
daughter Isabelle married Steven of Long Island.

The Conception

Al and I came straight home after the movies (Marilyn Monroe and Yves Montand in *Let's Make Love*), shared half a box of Yodels, and went to bed hoping to make a baby.

Afterwards, I got up and finished the Yodels.

After

The Pregnancy

I went to the doctor three weeks after I missed my period. The doctor thought I might be pregnant, but he needed to do a "rabbit test"—inject my urine into a healthy rabbit— to make sure. It was 1959, and that's what they did then.

When the test came back, I was joyous. The rabbit wasn't.

In those days, nobody could tell the sex of a baby until it was born. I wanted a girl. The only names I liked were Pamela, Jessica, and Victoria. (I watched a lot of soap operas.)

"Oh, John."   "Oh, Jessica."

Right from the start, I wanted my daughter's world to be perfect. I listened to *Excerpts from the World's Greatest Symphonies* with the speaker on my stomach.

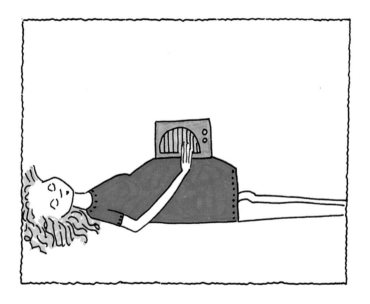

Beethoven's Fifth. My first.

I stopped reading *Cosmopolitan,* joined the Book-of-the-Month Club, and read aloud to my stomach.

I went to the Museum of Modern Art a lot. There was never a line in the ladies room.

I was going to be the perfect mother. I stopped smoking. I wore sensible shoes with arch support. I took Stuart's Prenatal Vitamins. I bought Dr. Spock's *The Common Sense Book of Baby and Child Care* in hardcover.

I was going to give my daughter all the mothering I'd missed because my mother had died when I was young. When she was young.

I was going to be the mother I always wanted to have—loving, understanding, optimistic, and fun. My daughter was going to be so happy.

She was going to be the daughter I always wanted to be—brilliant, artistic, beautiful, thin. I was going to be so happy.

We were both so lucky.

Lucky us.

May 27, 1960, I gave birth to a girl.

Every baby is a miracle. Every baby is beautiful. My daughter was even better than that.

M any years later, at eleven o'clock on a Friday night, my daughter flew into the house. "Mom, look!" she shouted and stuck out her left hand.

I saw a ring you wouldn't be afraid to wear on a subway.

"I'm engaged!" she shrieked and ran to the telephone.

I thought about my daughter—all the dancing lessons and piano lessons. The orthodontist and the dermatologist. The fancy summer camp that had horseback riding. Her junior year abroad. MasterCards and Visas. Bloomingdale's and Saks. Closets full of shoes.

I thought about my future son-in-law. He was tall. He did have nice hair. Was he good enough for her? How could he possibly be?

Spreading the news

I thought about the fairy tales I had read to my daughter when she was little—Cinderella, Snow White, Sleeping Beauty. There was always a Prince Charming.

I remembered reading about the Duke of Windsor abdicating his throne for Wallis Simpson in 1936. He said, "I have found it impossible to carry the heavy burden of responsibility and to discharge my duties as King without the help and support of the woman I love."

It was even more romantic than a fairy tale.

I wondered what Wallis had that my daughter didn't?

Wallis

I had always hoped my daughter would marry someone with initials after his last name.

Maxwell Harris, M.D., D.D.S., Ph.D., L.L.D.

Or Roman numerals.

Bradford Dudley Buxton III

Or someone who looked like Warren Beatty in *Splendor in the Grass.*

I asked my daughter what she and her fiancé would live on.

My grandmother had asked me the same question when I got engaged.

P lanning a wedding, I discovered, is similar to producing a show at a dinner-theater in New Jersey.

Both events have a script, stars, a supporting cast, and a budget that's too small. Both have critics to please.

Frank Rich and John Simon are pussycats compared with my cousin Esther from Fort Lauderdale and my husband's aunt Sarah from Brooklyn.

My daughter bought a wedding book. She read every word. Every day.

She wanted to follow every wedding tradition. Even the new ones.

Unimportant things became important. Should the invitations be in blue or black ink? Should the postage stamps be lovebirds or hearts? How should the napkins be folded?

My daughter consulted her book. I wondered which stamps Jacqueline Kennedy would have chosen.

I never went anywhere without lists, schedules, and budgets. Everything was critical. Everything was an emergency. Everything was overpriced.

Was there really a time when all a bride needed was a father with a cow?

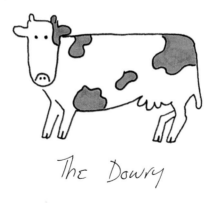

The Dowry

I didn't invite the groom's parents over; we needed a new couch. Instead we met at a restaurant. I felt confident. I was wearing beige.

"You have such a wonderful son," I said to his mother. Would my grandchildren look like her? I thought.

His mother started to say something about the wedding, but stopped, midsentence. Her son had given her a look that was familiar to me, a look my daughter frequently gave me.

All of a sudden, I liked her.

But when my daughter started getting very friendly with her mother-in-law-to-be, calling her more than she called me, asking her opinion more than she asked mine, I changed my mind.

Even King Solomon knew you can't have two mothers.

The groom's mother wanted the wedding close to where she lived so it wouldn't inconvenience her friends. I wanted it close to where I lived so it wouldn't inconvenience my friends. We compromised on a place midway between us. That way, everybody would be inconvenienced.

Mothers-in-law

My daughter said she wanted a simple wedding and handed me a list of things to do. During the next few days she added to the list. More days passed. More lists. I bought a two-inch-thick three-ring loose-leaf binder.

By the end of a week, I overheard her tell her friend, "My mother is driving me crazy. I need a wedding consultant."

My daughter found Deirdre, the perfect wedding consultant.

Wedding consultants take credit for everything good that happens. I feel responsible for everything bad that happens. I always wonder what I did wrong.

I never learned to pass the blame on to my mother. You're supposed to. Every psychology book says, "The cause of your problems is your mother."

It makes sense. Everybody has a mother.

What did I do wrong today?

Deirdre had a creative solution to every problem, even rain at a garden wedding. "A silk Moroccan tent, only $10,000! Isn't that fabulous!" Deirdre only spoke in exclamation points!

I think my daughter would have preferred a wedding consultant as a mother when she was growing up. Someone who could keep a pastel Dior scarf around her shoulders without tying a knot, and a flip in her hair without hair spray.

Someone who would never get upset or have a run in her stocking.

The Perfect Wedding

The Consultant

Deirdre told my daughter if she wanted custom-designed invitations, she was late ordering them.

Funny, I had wanted custom-designed announcements when my daughter was born, but I was too late ordering them. I settled on announcements from Woolworth's. I chose ones that had a pink bow that almost looked real and filled in the blanks with a pink pen I found in an art store.

The invitations came in packages of eight. I bought three packages and had six left over.

For her wedding, my daughter was going to need 400 invitations. The word *coronation* came to mind.

Announcing the arrival of

Name _____

Date _____

Weight _____

Happy parents

_____

Deirdre suggested a monogram on the invitation. I always thought monograms were only for rich people. My rich great-aunt Ethel had a monogram embroidered in the lining of her Persian lamb coat. The only reason she wasn't invited to the wedding was because she was dead.

I wonder what happened to her coat.

Great-Aunt Ethel

The wording of the wedding invitation presented some choices. I worried that Deirdre was going to suggest a consultation with another expert—maybe Letitia Baldrige.

When my daughter was little, I believed in experts. Dr. Spock's *Baby and Child Care* was my bible. So reassuring, so *laissez-faire*. "Trust yourself," it began. "You know more than you think."

Years later I think I read that Dr. Spock once said the only person he ever trusted was his domineering mother, Mildred.

Trust Yourself

1. **You know more than you think you do.** have a baby. Maybe you have one alrea excited, but if you haven't had much ex whether you are going to know how to you have been listening more careful relatives when they talk about bring begun to read articles by "experts" newspapers. After the baby is born, will begin to give you instructions to like a very complicated business vitamins a baby needs and all t mother tells you she couldn't live w another swears by cloth diapers. easily spoiled by being picked up

I didn't rely only on Dr. Spock. I read books by another expert, Haim G. Ginott. His advice was to find fault with the act, not with the person. If your child spills the milk, he advised, say, "It makes me angry when the milk is spilled. Let's clean it up."

Never say, "You always spill the milk. You're as clumsy as your father."

By the time my daughter was in school, I had stopped reading child psychology books. I was too busy being a mother.

All the parenting books had said, "Don't rush in with advice," but who else is going to tell a daughter she needs a slip under that dress?

One afternoon I went looking for a memory box I'd been keeping for my daughter. I found it on a back shelf in my closet, took it down, and looked through it.

Inside I found report cards, a dancing-school certificate, a baby tooth, a lock of curly blond hair, and some handmade Valentine's Day cards. I also found a letter my daughter had sent me from summer camp.

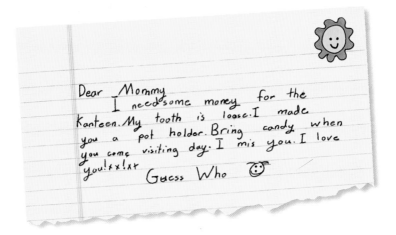

And a birthday letter she had sent me from college.

Dear Mom,
When you get really old, I promise
I will take care of you. I will
cook you prunes and farina, I will
buy you a pretty glass for your teeth,
I will let you win at gin rummy.
Happy Birthday!
Love and xxxxxxxx's
Your #1 daughter

The years between "Dear Mommy" and "Dear Mom" had gone by so fast.

It seemed like only yesterday that she was sitting on my lap watching Miss Barbara on *Romper Room*, Captain Kangaroo, and Mr. Rogers on our black-and-white TV.

The Captain   Mr. Rogers

When she started to walk, I bought her a tricycle. When she learned how to ride her tricycle, I got her a two-wheeler.

I didn't know how quickly she'd grow up.

Spaghetti O's

I wish I could go back to then, buy her pretty hair ribbons and barrettes, make her SpaghettiO's for lunch, see which one of us could scream the longest without taking a breath when we drove through the Lincoln Tunnel.

My daughter hasn't called me Mommy in a long time. But to this day, every time I hear a child say "Mommy" in the supermarket, I turn around.

I'm so full of memories.

How she cried, pulled at my skirt and wouldn't let go of me the first day of nursery school.

How she stood on a kitchen chair and sang all the words to every song in the third-grade play but was too shy to even move her lips on stage.

How she always had a Band-Aid on her knee.

I remember teaching her to dance. With her little feet on my big feet, we lindied and fox-trotted to Frank Sinatra and Sammy Davis Jr., singing "Me and My Shadow."

Me and my shadow

When my daughter was little, she thought I knew all the answers.She thought I could do everything. She thought I was wonderful. Her friends did, too. They always wanted to come to our house.

I let them finger-paint. I let them eat Yodels.

Finger painting

"You can be anything you want to be," I was always telling my daughter.

I bought her a PlaySkool doctor's kit and eagerly became her first patient.

I showed her how to build Lego skyscrapers.

Picasso couldn't have had more crayons or poster paints when he was growing up.

Picasso's
self-portrait?

My daughter's
self-portrait!

We bought her a piano from Macy's.
It took three years to pay off on the
installment plan. The piano lessons
lasted only two years.

Every spring I bought her another sequined
costume for her dancing-school recital.

Years later, I was always telling her,
"Clean your room, do your homework,
don't leave your dishes in the sink."

Reality had interrupted my dreams.

When my daughter was a toddler and didn't get what she wanted, she would lie down on the floor and scream.

When she got older, she sulked. I prefer the noise to the silence.

Everything was so easy when my daughter was little, even though I didn't think so at the time.

W hen did it all begin to change? When she was in junior high and started hanging out at the mall? If we went to the mall together, she didn't want me to hold her hand. "My friends might see," she said.

But at home, she'd climb into my bed and ask me to tickle her back while we watched *Dynasty*.

High school wasn't easy—for either of us. She complained that she had nothing to wear. I complained about her friends.

She groaned about her chest being too big and her hair being too flat. "I inherited all your genes," she told me. All her friends, she said, had fabulous figures, fabulous hair, and fabulous mothers. I groaned about her study habits.

She said that only nice guys asked her out, that nice guys were boring, and announced that she'd never marry a nice guy. I announced that she couldn't sleep over at the Jersey shore on prom night.

She told me that all I did was criticize. Even when I said nothing.

If you see a woman losing her mind in Shop Rite, you know she's the mother of a two-year-old or a teenager.

At ShopRite

When I was younger and did something that really exasperated my grandmother, she'd shake her finger at me and say, "I only pray to God that when you get married and have children, they're just like you."

God had answered her prayers.

Grandma

Audrey

I never wore a bridal gown. If I had, it would have been a fancy one with sparkles, satin roses, seed pearls, and lace insets.

Like most brides, my daughter wanted to look like Audrey Hepburn. The wedding dresses she liked looked like slips.

My daughter and I each bought our own copies of every bridal magazine. Every magazine had the same dresses, almost the same articles. We compared our choices over the phone.

> *"Do you have the Priscilla of Boston with the sweetheart illusion neckline?"* I'd ask.
>
> *"No. Go find the Vera Wang with the dropped waist and the lace tank top,"* she'd answer.

It reminded me of the summer she was seven and had the chicken pox. We played Go Fish constantly.

> *"Do you have any diamonds?"* I'd ask.
>
> *"Go fish. Do you have a heart?"* she'd answer.

We went to a bridal fashion show at
Bloomingdale's. The models were
very tall, very thin, and very flat.
They looked like bread sticks.

I caught a glimpse of myself in a mirror. I looked like a Kaiser roll.

I wanted my daughter to be proud of the way I looked at the wedding. I bought a leotard and a Jane Fonda exercise video. I watched the tape only once. It was too depressing.

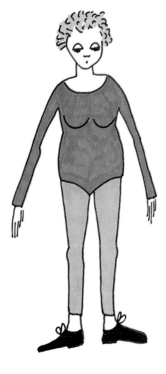

Too late for Jane

I stopped eating everything that tasted good. But I was happy. I was spending more time with my daughter than I had in years.

Happy

I had never shopped for a wedding dress before.

I thought *peau de soie* was something Julia Child made.
That Swarovski crystals were a rich person's gallstones.
That *charmeuse* was someone who sang like Edith Piaf.
That Alençon lace was a cheese people with bad
cholesterol could eat.

My daughter tried on a dress made from fifty yards of Thai
silk. I couldn't find her. She tried on a sheath covered with
fifty pounds of mother-of-pearl baguettes. She almost fell
over.

There was one thing we agreed on: no bows on the
derriere.

Looking

When I looked at my grown daughter trying on wedding dresses, I still saw a child.

Memories of being with her in other fitting rooms came back to me. I always thought everything looked beautiful on her. She never did.

Shopping

"Don't talk so loud," she'd say. *"Someone might hear."*

"What would they hear? My saying 'It looks gorgeous on you'"?

"Mom, it makes me look fat!"

Here we were years later. The salesgirl slipped a bias-cut satin bridal gown over my daughter's head.

"It looks gorgeous on you," I said.

"It makes me look fat," she said.

The salesgirl came in and out of the dressing room, each time her arms full of wedding-dress fluff. My daughter would take one look and shake her head.

"Just try them on," I said. "Maybe you'll like one."

I always said that to her when we went shopping.
We were always having the same conversation.

I was always saying to her:

> *"Because I'm your mother, that's why."*
> *"Take your hair out of your eyes."*
> *"Stand up straight."*
> *"With all the clothes you have,*
> * that's what you're wearing?"*
> *"Stop biting your nails."*
> *"Don't pick your face."*
> *"Call me when you get there."*

She was always saying to me:

"All my friends are going."
"You don't understand."
"I can't tell you anything."
"Sure you'd say that. You're my mother."
"It's not fair."
"You're ruining my life."
"Mom, get off my case."

The bridal department was on the seventh floor. We took the elevator up. A woman and a little girl got on at the fifth-floor toy department. The woman's glasses were held together on one side with tape, her roots needed a touch-up, and her brown loafers had seen a lot of rainy days. The little girl kept whining, "I want a toy. I want a toy."

I wanted to lean over and tell the woman these would be her happiest years.

That night, I was sitting in the kitchen with a Diet Coke and middle-aged spread. My daughter hadn't called for our nightly wedding conversation, so I called her.

"Are you still mad at me?" I asked. I had embarrassed her at Vera Wang's. All I said was, "Isn't she the most beautiful bride you ever saw?" Our salesgirl wasn't even Vera.

A few weeks and a dozen stores later, she found a dress she loved. I didn't think she ever would. But, when she was three, I didn't think she'd ever be toilet trained either.

Mad at me again

I didn't know anything about bridal accessories, but I had opinions.

Ava Gardner wore a hat when she married Mickey Rooney in 1942. They got divorced.

Rita Hayworth wore a hat when she married Orson Welles in 1943 (they got divorced); when she married Aly Khan in 1949 (they got divorced); and then Dick Haymes in 1953 (they got divorced).

Janet Leigh wore a hat when she married Tony Curtis in 1951. They got divorced.

Eddie and Liz

Even Eddie Fisher wore a hat when he married Elizabeth Taylor in 1959. And they got divorced.

I didn't think my daughter should wear a hat.

Or a tiara. Only Miss America or the Queen of England is entitled to a wear a tiara.

"Buy comfortable shoes," I advised my daughter. If your feet hurt, it doesn't even matter if you're marrying Prince William.

Miss America   Queen Elizabeth II

My daughter and I were so busy with wedding preparations, we'd forgotten about the shower.

"Do we really need a bridal shower?" I asked. She gave me the look—like lightning should strike me.

I spend a lot of time feeling guilty about things I've said to her. But she says I'm always laying a guilt trip on her.

What about the shaver?

Fathers never feel guilty. Fathers get television series like
Father Knows Best. They may worry about their sexual
performance, but they never worry about their
performance as a father.

Her father, a man of few words, had only one thing to say
about everything that was going on, but he said it a lot:
"And what are his parents paying for?"

My daughter's friends told her to register at the fancy department stores. We looked at crystal stemware. "You'll never use it," I told her. "Get good pots."

When I was my daughter's age, with a three-year-old playing with the garbage in the kitchen, a two-year old screaming in a playpen, and an infant spitting up on my shoulder, stemware wasn't what I needed.

We looked at silver patterns. "Let's check out the vacuum cleaners," I said. "I always wanted a great vacuum cleaner."

"I'm not you," my daughter said.

"Which pickle dish do you like?" my daughter asked me.

"You really need a pickle dish?" I asked her. I stopped myself from saying anything about children in Third World countries who never even saw a pickle.

I thought about my own mother. I can still hear the sound of her voice. "Eat! Eat! There are children starving in Europe."

Eat!

As a child, I didn't like to eat. Whatever my mother made, I hated.

"Eat! Eat!" she'd keep yelling.

"No, I won't," I'd yell back and accidentally on purpose spill my chocolate milk as I mumbled, "I hope you die."

You can say that to your mother. You'll feel guilty for the rest of your life, but your mother always loves you. No matter what you say or do. Even if you wish lightning would strike her.

No one will ever love you
more than your mother.
Not even your dog.

More and more my daughter was saying to me, "Mom, stop telling me what to get. You don't know everything."

I had an insight on the seventh floor of Bloomingdale's, right next to the Limoges boxes. When I was growing up, Eleanor Roosevelt and Shirley Temple were my role models. When my daughter was growing up, Bette Midler and Cher were her role models. No wonder we were different.

Why should my daughter be the way I was? I wasn't even the way I wanted to be.

Eleanor

Bette

No mother ever wants to admit being wrong. No daughter can ever grow up if her mother is right all the time.

I had to stop telling my daughter what to do and how to do it. I had to stop doing the dishes she left in the sink when I was in her apartment.

Her dishes weren't really any of my business anymore.

Not my business

When you're little, everything is your mother's business.

I remember when I was four, my mother made me wear leggings under my skirt and galoshes over my shoes if it was cold out.

One snowy day, I ran out of the house before she could get them on me. The next day, I came down with a temperature of 102° and a bad cough.

"You see," my mother said, "you shouldn't have gone out without your leggings and galoshes. You should have listened to me. I know what's best for you."

When you're four, your mother is usually right.

I understand my mother better now. I always think
I know what's best for my daughter.

Weddings, like daughters, can give you a headache. There were so many choices. There was the way my daughter wanted things, the way the groom wanted things. The way I thought things should be, the way the groom's mother thought they should be. There were the recommendations of her friends, the bridal books—and Deirdre.

Which cake? Which menu? Which photographer? Just color photos or black and white, too? The bridal bouquet, the bridesmaids' bouquets, boutonnieres, table centerpieces, color schemes, place cards, seating arrangements, music, bridesmaids' and groomsmen's gifts, thank-you cards—all were issues.

Did Elizabeth Taylor's mother go through this each time her daughter got married?

If only the first baby could be born second. As parents of a first child, we were so thrilled, so proud, so inexperienced, so terrified.

We celebrated our baby's every move. No wonder our first daughter grew up thinking the world would rejoice every time she sneezed.

We couldn't wait to have another baby.

"When is the new baby coming? When is the new baby going to be here?" my daughter asked as she kissed my big tummy.

One week after her sister arrived, she asked, "When is the new baby going back?"

Sibling rivalry had entered our happy home.

She'd ask, "Who is your favorite daughter? Who is your very favorite?" "You are my favorite first child," I'd answer. "Your sister is my favorite second child." I read that in a book.

I asked my friend Judy if there was sibling rivalry between her daughters. "No," she said. "They just naturally dislike each other."

As the wedding day grew closer, the sisters grew more apart. "If I have to spend one more minute talking about her wedding plans," I heard her sister say, "I'll tell the whole world she used to pick her nose and eat it."

Siblings

My daughter and I consulted with specialists in wedding music, authorities on champagne, experts on floral arrangements. I thought you only conferred with consultants when you had something like tax problems or gum disease.

Several of these people had no daytime hours. I remember having to miss the first two hours of the Academy Awards broadcast to meet with a string quartet.

String quartet

What do five girls—one short, one tall, one buxom, one flat, one who gave birth a month ago—have in common? A bridesmaid's dress they all hate.

My daughter wanted to keep her bridesmaids as friends. She had to find a dress that would look good on all of them, that they could wear again, and that wouldn't cost a lot. Finding the Holy Grail is easier.

Bridesmaids

Better than Entenmann's?

Fifteen hundred dollars for a wedding cake? I could have
a lifetime supply of Entenmann's chocolate doughnuts!

I should have stayed in the kitchen and become rich
making wedding cakes instead of learning to type.
Who knew.

My grandmother said she could have bought Coca-Cola
stock when it was fifty cents a share. Who knew.

M arriages may not last, but photographs do. My entire wedding cost as much as my daughter was going to spend on photographs.

When I was growing up, Bradford Bachrach took all the wedding photos of society people, the Rockefellers and the Roosevelts. I mentioned Bachrach to my daughter. She thought he wrote "Alfie."

I wanted to come out looking good in the pictures, so I wouldn't have to cut my face out of a group shot, which I did most of the time. I read that Claudette Colbert let photographers shoot only her left profile, her good side. I don't have a good side.

A wedding video? Who could resist? Love preserved forever on the screen. We met with a videographer. "Would you like the *When Harry Met Sally* treatment? We could throw in some home movies, love letters, and Gershwin songs. Or the more formal 'Her Serene Highness Grace Kelly marries Prince Rainer' look? Perhaps you'd like a PBS-type documentary?"

I remember saving S&H green stamps to buy an 8-mm camera so we could film my daughter's fifth birthday. The camera had no sound. My mother-in-law bought us the movie projector and folding screen. She kept them at her house.

Every time we went over to watch our movies, my mother-in-law said the same things: Shirley Temple couldn't hold a candle to her granddaughter; Cecile B. DeMille could learn a lot about moviemaking from her son; and what was I feeding them because they both looked so thin.

Cuter than Shirley Temple?

Mamie

When I was younger, ladies wore orchid corsages on special occasions. I asked the floral consultant about wearing an orchid corsage. He said not since Mamie Eisenhower could anyone get away with that.

Billie

I asked him about wearing a gardenia in my hair. He said I was more like Mamie Eisenhower than Billie Holiday and suggested I might want to carry a single rose. I wondered if I reminded him of Gertrude Stein.

Me?

I asked if the bridesmaids could carry daisies. From the look on his face, you'd have thought I said dandelions. Only Martha Stewart can get away with that.

The right music, everybody told us, could make
or break the wedding.

I saw an ad that said the Lester Lanin Orchestra played
at the reception of Prince Charles and Princess Diana,
the Duke and Duchess of York, Billy Joel and Christie
Brinkley. I called and asked if they ever played at
weddings for couples who stayed together.

One Monday morning, my daughter called. "Mom, why did you tell Deirdre I'm driving you crazy, the wedding is becoming ridiculous, and you wish we'd elope or break up?"

"I was joking," I said.

"No you weren't," she said and hung up the telephone.

The wedding preparations were bringing out the worst in both of us.

Maternal devotion is supposed to be stronger than superglue. It's against nature to say that your children expect too much of you. But tell anybody, including the checkout girl at Shop Rite, that your husband expects too much of you, nobody even raises an eyebrow.

Being a mother used to be so easy. All I needed to make my daughter happy was a box of Mallomars or some Silly Putty.

I wanted my daughter to be happy. "Well, just as long as you're happy," I'd say.

I said it to her when I was embarrassed because she wouldn't wear anything but her Halloween costume to nursery school for weeks.

Just like Bo (with braces)

I said it to her when she had her hair braided like Bo Derek in *Ten* and I knew she was having trouble sleeping on the beads.

I said it to her about the college she chose.

I said it to her when she got engaged.

I was lying. What I really wanted was for the things that made me happy to make her happy.

At least I wasn't like my friend Sheila. Every Christmas we had to go see her daughter in *The Nutcracker*, because Sheila always wanted to be a ballerina.

One night I woke up around 3 A.M., got out of bed, and wrote a letter to my daughter.

Darling,

I never knew before I had you that I could love anyone so much. You won't understand the feeling until you hold your own baby in your arms.

I'm afraid you won't need me now that you're married. I helped you get over your separation anxiety in nursery school. Now I need you to help me get over mine.

I never sent the letter.

I was feeling so unnecessary. I had gone from being a powerless daughter to a powerless wife to a powerless mother—all too quickly.

I had been so busy changing diapers, I didn't have time to read *The Feminine Mystique.* I had been so busy trying to look like Gloria Steinem, I didn't have time to read Gloria Steinem.

Women of my generation thought our children were our careers. Most of us didn't know we could be anything else. When I was in my twenties, you were just supposed to get married. I never had to say, "I'm just a housewife."

I never regretted not having a career. You only get a few years to be the mother of young children.

But girls today want a lot more.

And they expect a lot from their mothers.

There's never been a Mothers' Movement. Nobody ever thought about passing legislation to end the impossible expectations children have of mothers.

Mothers have no advocates. Maybe Shakespeare was
thinking about mothers when he wrote:

> *If you prick us do we not bleed? If you tickle us,*
> *do we not laugh? If you poison us, do we not die?*

Maybe Arthur Miller should have written "Attention must
be paid" about mothers.

One afternoon, the bride- and groom-to-be and I were going over the wedding menu.

The hors d'oeuvres suggestions included saffron and black sesame crepes filled with julienne vegetable curry, seared tuna on a potato crisp, medallion of lobster with salmon eggs, taramasalata with pita bread, roulade of smoked duck breast and duck-liver mousse.

I suggested they also include a tray of Tums and Rolaids.

"When your father and I were married at your grandmother's house in Queens," I said, "we served deli platters. Everybody loved them. Especially your uncle Harold. He kept count on the miniature hot dogs and didn't allow anyone more than three."

"Mom, you want me to have pigs-in-a-blanket in the living room?"

"Of course not, honey," I said. "You take everything I do or say the wrong way. I was just remembering."

The groom-to-be took my daughter's hand and kissed it. "Don't be so touchy," he said. "Your mother didn't mean anything." More and more I was getting to like this young man.

I didn't know how to act with my daughter anymore. I had to watch my words. I had to watch my tone of voice. Once she was inside my body. Now I was getting under her skin.

My daughter didn't understand that the umbilical cord that had attached us for nine months came with a lifetime warranty. That even before the original one had dried up and fallen off, I'd already macraméd another.

There was no part of my daughter that I didn't know, hadn't washed, hadn't kissed. Now she was annoyed when I brushed her hair back out of her eyes.

I once heard my grandmother say, "To a ninety-five-year-old mother, her seventy-year-old daughter is still her baby."

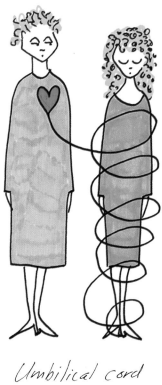

Umbilical cord

My friend Dora says I overidentify with my daughter. Maybe I do. When my daughter had a bad dream, I couldn't sleep. When she had the chicken pox, I itched. When she sneezed, I blew. When she got her period, I had cramps.

I worried about her book reports, her driving test, her SATs, her boyfriends, her job interviews. I thought that's what it meant to be a good mother.

My daughter says she can't tell me the truth about anything because I worry.

If she tells me she's having problems with her job, she says I'll worry she's about to get fired. If she tells me she's having problems with her fiancé, I'll worry that they're going to break up.

I bought a book about problems between mothers and adult daughters. I read the first chapter and worried about everything I did wrong.

My daughter thinks she knows everything about me. She thinks she knows what I'm going to say before I say it. Sometimes she's right.

Sooner or later, she knows I'll come up with the Horror Story.

About a girl who didn't take care of a mole on her face and it turned into leprosy.

About another girl who disappeared after a party in the East Village and turned up months later as part of a white slave ring in the Middle East.

About Jean Harlow who bleached her hair so much she died of peroxide poisoning.

Harlow

But I also told my daughter inspiring things.

About my dental hygienist's third cousin everybody thought was a loser in high school who became the head of a big movie studio in Hollywood and who knows Warren Beatty.

About my niece who bought a mansion in Greenwich, and found an Armani suit for half price at Loehmann's.

About a girl who was in her Brownie troop in elementary school, who got a law degree and a medical degree from Harvard and passed her psychiatry boards all in the same year, while working part time at the Kinney shoe store.

Imagine having a doctor and lawyer in the family!

But who needs a psychiatrist when they have a mother?

If there's one thing my daughter doesn't need, it's a psychiatrist. Why should she waste money talking to a stranger when I've known her all her life?

I finally had to face the prospect of what I would wear to the wedding. Mother-of-the-bride dresses over size 12 look like something Mrs. Krushchev would wear. But I couldn't put it off anymore. I had to look for a dress.

I wondered what Jackie O. would wear. I always wondered what Jackie O. would wear, even though she was built like an ironing board and I looked more like an upholstered chair.

I tried on a pale pink and violet Monet-like chiffon print.
Ladybird Johnson would have loved it. I looked like a field
of wildflowers.

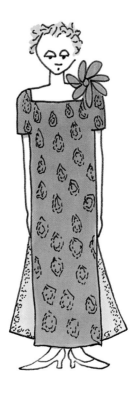

I tried on turquoise crepe. I looked like a wall in a
hospital.

I tried on blue sequins. I looked like the aurora borealis.

All-white weddings were big that year. I tried on white moiré. I looked like the Pillsbury Doughboy.

I tried on green velvet. A Rodney Dangerfield line came to me: "If that dress had pockets, you'd look like a pool table." The dress had pockets.

I finally found something. It showed a little cleavage.
I learned a long time ago, if you show a little cleavage,
nobody ever looks anywhere else.

Nobody pays attention to what the mother of the bride is wearing anyway.

Everybody remembers Princess Diana's wedding dress, but who remembers what her mother wore?

Nobody pays attention to the mother of the bride.

I never told my daughter about the birds and the bees. She just knew. Probably from her friend Sheryl. Nobody told me about the birds and the bees. I found out from my friend Babs.

But now that my daughter was getting married, I thought I should give her advice:

> *Wearing a sexy nightgown to bed is more important than having a clean kitchen floor.*

> *Compliment your husband frequently. Even if it's not true, he'll believe you.*

> *Always have some leftovers in the refrigerator, even if you have to buy them.*

I wish I'd followed my own advice.

Maybe I should have said what my grandmother said to me. Nothing. But then I never saw my grandmother and grandfather kiss. When I was growing up, I never saw anybody kiss except in the movies.

But my daughter's generation had very different ideas about marriage than my generation had. As different as my ideas were from my grandmother's.

My grandmother wanted security. I wanted love. My daughter wanted security, love, and everything else she thought she was entitled to.

My daughter suggested we make an appointment for a professional beauty day just before the wedding. "We can get a massage, a manicure, a pedicure, and relax," she said. It was hard for me to relax when I found out how much our day of beauty cost.

The morning of our day of beauty, I looked in the mirror. I was going to need more than a day.

Needs work

The Saturday night before the wedding, channel 2's weather report said sunny skies for Sunday. Sunday, we woke up to showers.

I looked at myself in the bathroom mirror. Beauty day had been a waste of money.

The wedding was at four. We had decided to dress at the country club because it would be quiet. We got there at two o'clock. The photographer, the flower lady, the video people, the caterer, the groom's mother, several children, the string quartet, and a couple of aunts were already there.

I heard someone say, "I can't do a thing with my hair," and someone answer, "Your hair looks fabulous." The bridesmaids had arrived.

One of them put on a tape. Carly Simon started singing "You're So Vain." There was girl stuff all around—blow dryers, strapless bras, mascara, lip gloss, panty hose, earrings, tampons, eye shadows, ponytail holders. And girl smells—hair spray, toothpaste, mouthwash, deodorant, White Linen, L'Air du Temps.

The bridesmaids whispered to one another about the awful weather and told the bride rain meant good luck.

All of a sudden, it was quarter to four. I looked out the window. The rain had stopped.

I don't remember walking down the aisle but I heard the quartet play "Here Comes the Bride," and I saw my daughter walking down the aisle on her father's arm.

Halfway to the altar, her father raised her veil and kissed her cheek. The groom walked toward her, took her hand, and together bride and groom continued walking down the aisle.

Just like in the movies. But better.

My daughter was Cinderella, Snow White, Grace Kelly, Audrey Hepburn, and Jacqueline Kennedy. But better.

And the man at her side *was* Prince Charming.

My daughter and her prince

The ceremony was over, but I hadn't heard a word.
All I could think about was that my little girl was
now someone's wife.

I remembered hearing someone say—I think it was on
As the World Turns—"The days go by so slowly, the years
so fast."

Now here I was standing next to my daughter in a receiving line.

People with familiar and unfamiliar faces kept shaking my hand, kissing my cheek.

"Everything is lovely," they said. "And you look wonderful." I started to believe them. I started to feel like a movie star, someone serene and elegant like Deborah Kerr.

Receiving

Then I went into the bathroom and looked in the mirror. I had lipstick all over my face from the kisses and my mascara was smudged.

Life is never like the movies.

The receiving line moved slowly.

Then all of a sudden, everything was speeding up— champagne toasts, dinner, dancing. I felt like I was watching one of those MTV videos where twenty years is compressed into twenty seconds.

I looked around at my relatives.

I shouldn't have expected Aunt Sarah to like anything. Not after being married to my uncle Harold for forty years. She didn't like her table even more than she didn't like the hors d'oeuvres. She asked me why my hair was in my eyes and why I'd wear a dress with a neckline that showed so much.

"If you can't say something nice about somebody, sit by me," Alice Roosevelt Longworth said a long time ago. She must have heard it from my aunt Sarah.

My aunt Betty thought the band was too loud. Her husband said they didn't play any rumbas. Cousin Ann didn't like the chicken. Her husband agreed and said the portions were too small. Rose and George thought they should be at a better table. The people at their table wanted to be at a better table.

The family

I had a little champagne. I felt wonderful for about five minutes, and then I thought about after the wedding. My son-in-law would be bringing my daughter Mallomars, not me.

What would I do? What could I look forward to? My daughter's marriage was just starting. Mine was deteriorating. She had babies to look forward to. I had chin hairs and calcium deficiency ahead of me.

I thought about being a
grandmother. Impossible.

Grandmothers cooked chicken soup
and knitted sweaters. I didn't know
how to do either.

I was the mother. How could my
baby have a baby?

Not yet

Somebody once said—maybe it was on *General Hospital*— "A woman has daughters so somebody will need her." She doesn't know until she gets older how much she needs them.

Just before the wedding was over, my daughter went to the microphone. She spoke softly, "Instead of throwing the bridal bouquet, I want to give it to my mother and thank her for always being there for me."

There were tears in her eyes. And in mine.

Nothing is easy. Not even happiness.

Four hours later

The year of planning had resulted in a ceremony that lasted twenty minutes and a reception that was over in four hours. But I'd do it all over again in a heartbeat.

As a mother-in-law, I became someone who sees no evil, hears no evil, and speaks no evil.

And I made other changes, too. I gained back the weight I lost, and I transferred all the wedding bills to charge cards with lower interest rates.

The perfect mother-in-law

Three months after the wedding, my daughter was still sending out thank-you notes for gifts.

The best gift I ever received was my daughter. Maybe I should have sent a thank-you note.

Even with the aggravation, worry, headaches, and sleepless nights, being a mother is the best part of my life.

Five months after the wedding, the pictures were ready. When I looked at them, I didn't think I looked as bad as I might have—but I didn't look as good as I'd hoped.

I put one of the pictures of my daughter and son-in-law in an ornate gold frame on my coffee table. The frame was a wedding present my daughter didn't like. I didn't like it much either.